G000078049

To:

From:

My Little One

Becky Kelly

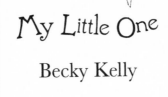

**Andrews McMeel
Publishing, LLC**

Kansas City

08 09 10 11 12 LEO 10 9 8 7 6 5 4 3 2 1

ISBN-13: 978-0-7407-7389-1
ISBN-10: 0-7407-7389-5

Library of Congress Control Number: 2008922965

www.andrewsmcmeel.com

ATTENTION: SCHOOLS AND BUSINESSES
Andrews McMeel books are available at quantity discounts
with bulk purchase for educational, business, or sales
promotional use. For information, please write to:
Special Sales Department, Andrews McMeel Publishing, LLC,
1130 Walnut Street, Kansas City, Missouri 64106.

For Little Kate

My little one . . .
sent from up above.

Cradled gently

in my arms . . .

surrounded by love.

Itty-bitty fingers,
teeny-tiny toes,

sweet, chubby cheeks
. . . bitty baby nose.

Warm as a kitten . . .
soft as a breeze,

my little one kicks
with chubby baby knees.

My little one,
my bundle of joy . . .
the apple of my eye.

You sing the song
that awakens my heart,
my sweet potato pie.

My little one

sent to me . . .

as you wrap your finger
around my heart,
I dream of what could be.

Might you be a sweet one?

Or will you be a star?

Or will you be an ornery one
and drive a red sports car?

Will you be a doctor
or will you
be a nurse . . .

or will you fly a plane . . .

or will you be a cowboy
and ride the open range?

Welcome to
this big world . . .
my little one, my love.

You fill my days
and bless my nights
with dreams from up above.

My little one,
my wonder . . .
cradled deep within my heart,

always know that
you are loved,
right from the very start.